Divided by Witchcraft

A Pendle Witch Short Story

Inspired by the True Story of the Samlesbury Witches

Karen Perkins

LionheART Publishing House

Author's Note

To reflect the setting and characters of 17th-century Lancashire, a flavour of the dialect is used in the dialogue and narrative, for example:

Allus (always)
Frit (fright/frightened)
Gronny (granny)
Hersen/Hissen/Mesen (herself/himself/myself)
Nowt (nothing)
Reet (right)
Sennight (week)
Summat (something)

Witches should be killed whether they have murdered anyone with a magical herb or poison, or not; and whether they have done harm to crops or creatures, or not.

Martín del Rio – Jesuit Priest and Witch Hunter

Divided by Witchcraft
A Pendle Witch Short Story

Inspired by the True Story of the Samlesbury Witches

Chapter 1

Sunday, 5th April 1612

I couldn't understand what all the fuss were about. It were a bit more interesting to hear the words in English instead of Latin, reet enough, but St. Leonard-the-Less were so bare! No bugger cracked a smile, and all the dour faces and plain clothes were, well . . . less. The church had been named well; there'd been nowt to look at, and the words just droned on after a bit.

Why were Mam fighting so hard with Gronny Jennet and Aunt Ellen over which church to sit in? Folk just like to do things their own way, that's all. God were the same wherever we sat, weren't He?

'What evil is this?'

I blinked in the sunshine and stopped short at the words. That were Mam's voice. Bugger, I were for it now, reet enough. I shrank back into Aunt Ellen's side, but nowt could save me.

The tall, stooped man standing with Mam spoke, and I gasped as I recognised Father Christopher. No, wait, I weren't to call him Father Christopher, nor

Southworth for that matter. Master Thomson, that were it. Thomson were the name we were supposed to call him.

'Grace Sowerbutts! Don't be so rude, daughter. Listen when you are spoken to!' I felt heat in me face at Mam's rebuke as I realised the Father had been talking and I'd heard nowt of his words.

He blew out a breath in frustration. 'Young Grace, I am sorely disappointed in you. You betray not only your family, but your faith, your Lord God, and your Saviour.'

I stared at him. He had the loudest voice I'd ever heard. He looked about him, then took me arm and led me down the lane where it were more secluded. I heard Mam chiding Gronny and Aunt Ellen as they followed.

The Father lowered his voice. 'When I was told about the proliferation of witchcraft and the Devil's works in this great County of Lancaster, I did not expect to find such wickedness so close to home.' He looked up, staring past me. 'Not only amongst my brother's tenants, but by own nephew's widow!'

I started as his voice rose once more and glanced round. Aunt Ellen's friend, Mistress Jane, were glaring at him with such ferocity, I couldn't decide if she were vexed, frit or just hated the Father. Mebbe a bit of each.

She walked towards us. 'Christopher,' she said. 'It is not like you to visit the true Church of England.'

I stared at the Father in amazement. He'd turned a very odd colour, one I'd never seen on a man's face afore. Not even Pa's when he found me with Stevie Armstrong int' hayloft.

'How dare you,' he hissed.

'I follow the true religion of our King, and of our Queen before him,' she said, and I stared in amazement at her daring to speak to him like this.

'You have betrayed your true faith,' the Father continued. 'Witch!'

Mistress Jane stared at him. 'So it is true then. You *are* behind the rumours. I had been told as much, but could not believe you would so malign your dear nephew as to slander his widow with such blasphemy.'

'You are the blasphemer, not I. You and your friends here.' He pointed at Gronny Jennet and Aunt Ellen. 'And if that were not enough, you are blackening innocent souls.'

He grabbed hold of me arm, and I squealed in protest. I looked ower at Mam for help, but she were glaring at Aunt Ellen. There'd be hell to pay for me sneaking off with 'em, why ever had I listened to Gronny?

'Well, I promise you, you shall not have this young soul, and I shall do everything in my power to ensure you do not spread the Devil's corruption any further. I shall stop you, Mistress. All of you.' He glared once more at the three women, then whirled about, still clutching me arm, and pulled me along the lane.

'Mam!' I cried, and she looked at me, stretched out a finger to hook the curl of hair I'd been sucking on, out of me mouth in a quick movement, then took me other arm.

'Don't dawdle, Grace. You disobeyed me. I told you not to go with your aunt and gronny. I warned you against visiting their church. Father Southworth—'

'Mistress Sowerbutts!'

'Begging your pardon, Father – er, Master Thomson.'

The Father nodded, but I noticed the colour in his thin face were still high.

'Master Thomson has kindly agreed to learn you your prayers.'

The Father winced. 'I shall *teach* you your prayers, Grace, and you shall learn well.'

Now it were Mam's turn to colour.

'The coming week is the most important time of the year, Grace, you know that don't you?'

I nodded. I knew today were Palm Sunday, with Holy Week coming up. The last week of Lent. In seven days we could eat meat again. It had been far too long since me last taste.

'You shall visit me regularly for spiritual instruction and tutelage.'

I stared at him, then glanced at Mam, dumbfounded to see her nodding. Surely she would not do this to me?

She briefly bowed her head. 'I thank you, Father,

4

but I fear we cannot pay for that much learning. As you know, we are but tenants of your good brother, Master Thomas, and this has not been a good spring for anyone working the land.'

'Hush, Mistress, there will be no cost to you, this is my solemn duty. It may not be too late for her soul; she may not yet be a demoniac. I shall rid her of the malign influences she has been subjected to, and you, my girl, shall vow to never succumb again to the promise of false worship.'

I nodded me agreement, knowing by the strength of Mam's grip on me arm that I could do nowt but agree.

Christopher Southworth tightened his lips into summat akin to a smile. 'That is good. It shall be my pleasure – no, my honour – to save such a promising young mistress from the encroaching evils of Protestants and witches.'

Chapter 2

Saturday 11th April 1612

Father Christopher stared at me from his seat next to the east wall of the hall. Not the parish church that Gronny Jennet and Aunt Ellen went to, o'course, but the longer walk to the chapel in Samlesbury Hall with Mam and Pa to sit the Easter Vigil.

The Father took a moment to meet the eyes of the faithful gathered in his ancestral home, and looked pleased to see so many here, then he looked at me again and gave me a small smile of approval. He were pleased with me learning, he'd told me so.

'We have heard the Liturgy of the Word many times in recent days. We have talked about how our Lord Jesus Christ was betrayed by Judas – one of his own men; his family – just as the one true faith has since been betrayed by Luther, Calvin and yes, I'm sad to say, even our own misguided King James.' His voice echoed in the rafters and reverberated around the large, dark-panelled hall. It were much more interesting here than at Aunt Ellen's church int' village.

'Christ went to his death, just as our great

monasteries and houses of faith were fatally devastated. Our monks, priests and all the people who relied on them, no, *depended* on them for absolution, for work, for physick, even for alms, were cast asunder. How many of these good men died on the gallows or atop heretical pyres? How many others and their families died of hunger, of sickness, or poverty? How many of *your* family have suffered as a result of this devastation, this mockery of faith?'

He paused for breath, the fervent colour in his usually pale cheeks fading as he glared around the hall. I shifted in me seat, uneasy now under his gaze.

He stood, took a breath, and his voice thundered from his gaunt frame once more. 'But there is yet hope! On this day, in this week, as we hold vigil for Christ's suffering and resurrection, the very night when Christ rose again, saving us all with his sacrifice, we must also rise, we must also sacrifice.' His voice hushed. 'We must also save those who cannot save themselves. We must bring them back to God and the true faith.'

The hall were silent, and the Father stepped forward to walk among his congregation, and spoke more calmly. I sighed. This could go on for some time: dawn were yet a long way off.

'Most of you know my history. You have heard of how, as a young man, I fled the heretic queen to join the English College at Douai in France to pledge my life to the return of the true faith to this newly heathen land.

'I travelled to Rome, to continue my studies at the Jesuit College and to be ordained into the priesthood. Then I left that fine, devout and pious city to risk my life in returning to these shores, despite the dangers.'

He had reached the far end of the chapel, below the gallery where those of his family who were still Catholic sat in privacy and overlooked the rest of us. He turned, then walked down the closer aisle, touching shoulders in greeting as he went. I jumped when his voice filled the rafters once more.

'I have paid a heavy price for my faith, and have paid it gladly. I have spent many years in many gaols, endured many hardships, yet it has only served to strengthen my faith and my commitment to God.

'And when King James, in his wisdom, ordered priests of the true faith into exile, I was able to secrete myself in this good county and am finally able to do the work for which Our Lord chose me—'

He'd reached the front of the hall again, and spun, his crimson robes swirling around his lanky legs, and raised his arms.

'To bring hope! To bring light to this lost land! To bring you the true body and blood of Christ, and to bring you salvation and true absolution!'

He lowered his arms as his last words echoed above. I was unable to take me eyes from him, and nobody made a sound as we waited for his next words.

'Yet there are even greater dangers than mockery of the true faith.' He cast his eyes about the hall.

'You all know what I'm talking about . . . witchcraft!'

He stooped and opened his arms out to us all.

'That is right, good people. Witchcraft. Right. Here. In. Lancashire.'

I winced with every word, I could do nowt to still mesen.

'None of us are safe. They can be found anywhere; even, I am sad to say, in my own family. That's right, my own brother's daughter-in-law is one of these handmaidens of the Devil. And, worse still, she is mother to another Southworth.'

He waited for the murmuring to cease then nodded his head.

'Yes, the Devil has my nephew within reach, but I shall not let him have the boy, oh no!'

I jumped at his shout.

'I shall save that boy's soul, have no fear of that.'

He glared around the hall, and I'm sure none doubted him.

'But it is not just my family. There is at least one other affected by this scourge, that of my very own student, Grace.'

I turned the red of a robin's breast as he pointed at me, and tried to sink into the bench. Mam pulled away so I couldn't hide in her side, and she hooked the curl of dark hair from me mouth as every bugger watched. I could feel the pricking of tears at the unwanted notice.

'But have no fear, she is also in my care. And you must take heed of those in *your* care.' He turned his gaze around the hall once more. '*You* must save the souls of those *you* love. But fear not, for I am here to aid you in your Godly endeavours.'

Chapter 3

Monday 13th April 1612

'It was good to see you so much at Samlesbury Hall over Easter, Grace. Have you carried out the penances I prescribed for your transgression?'

'Aye, Father.' I reckoned he were asking if I'd been saying all them Hail Marys and Our Fathers, and doing all them extra chores he'd told Mam to give me, *and* a ruddy fast. And I had. Most of 'em.

'Master!'

I jumped at his roar. 'Aye, Master.' I shrank into me chair and he took a deep breath to steady hissen, then spoke calmly.

'You understand that the first thing a woman does when becoming a witch is to turn from the faith?'

I nodded. He'd been telling me that a lot.

'Who does that remind you of?'

'Gronny Jennet and Aunt Ellen. Not me, they dragged me to St Leonard's, they did. They're me elders and they ignored me mam and took me against me will.'

'So you believe your aunt and grandmother to be witches?'

11

'Aye. Master, it's true, they're witches and they tried to make me a witch too!'

'And . . . my niece. Mistress Jane. She is together with them often?'

'Aye.'

'So tell me again what they have done to you.'

'Well, Father—'

'Master, Grace, do not forget again. It is very important that you call me Master Thomson. Do not let *anyone* hear you refer to me as Father.'

'Begging your pardon, Fa— Master.' I felt heat in me cheeks, and rushed on before he could punish me further. 'Well, Gronny—'

'That is, your grandmother, Jennet Bierley?'

'Aye Master, me gronny, well, she can turn hersen into a black dog. *And* she tried to make me jump int' water to die. Witches do that you know, they kill young uns in water.'

'Now Grace, you can tell a story better than that. Start with her turning into a dog, and don't leave anything out.'

I gulped, and a twinge pulled on me heart. I curled a lock of hair into me mouth, but took it out again reet quick at his frown. This were Gronny and Aunt Ellen's doing. If they hadn't made me go to their church, I wouldn't have had to have all these lessons with the Father since. I'd been working int' fields or sat here learning me prayers for more than a sennight now, having to watch Sarah Pickles and Stevie Armstrong go off together, giggling as they walked away from me. He were bound to go for her now, and it were all Gronny's fault!

'Well, Master, I've been tormented and vexed by Gronny and Aunt Ellen for years, I have. Aye and Owd Doewise too.'

'Old Doewise?'

'Aye, she's a friend of Gronny's. Half-blind she is and with a fearsome temper. Don't leave her cottage much now.'

The Father waved his hand as if waving Owd Doewise hersen away, though she were not here. 'Tell me what your grandmother has done.'

'Well, a while back—'

'How long is a while?'

I thought on it. 'Mebbe a month?'

'Are you asking me or telling me?'

'It were a month past, Master.' I glanced up at him and he seemed happy with that so I went on. 'Well, I passed Gronny Jennet on me way to Two Briggs to meet the ferry across the Ribble, and she looked like hersen, she did, and then I looked back and she were a dog, a big black un. Anyroad, she leapt at me and knocked me off a stile, and then ran off.'

'Were you injured?'

'Nay, Fa— Master.'

He frowned at me slip and I cast me eyes down again.

'And you are sure this dog was your grandmother, Jennet Bierley?'

I looked up again, relieved I were not in trouble

13

for nearly calling him wrong again. 'Aye, Master.' I beamed at him. I'd got it reet. 'It were her all reet. One minute she looked like Gronny, then when I looked again she were a black dog. Fearsome, she were.'

Father Southworth bent his head once, his lips pursed. 'I see. And what else?'

'Well . . .' I looked up at the ceiling while I thought. I remembered mesen and carried on with me tale. 'Well, there were another time when I were again off to Two Briggs. I were meeting me mam who'd been to Preston market. I thought she might have a treat for me; you know, a bit of ribbon for me hair, or mebbe even an orange. And I met Gronny again and it were the same as before.'

'So, in her own shape and then that of a black dog?'

'Aye, Master.' I had a flash of an idea. 'Only she weren't just any black dog, she were a black dog up on two legs.'

The Father raised his eyebrows in interest. He liked that. I carried on.

'Well, I weren't gonna take her to me mam looking like that, so I went across the fields, with her chasing me, till we came to a pond.'

'Which pond?'

'Int' fields between our cottage and the river. A big one it is, reeds all round the bank.'

The Father nodded, he knew which one I were

describing; it weren't far from John Singleton's cottage, where I came for me lessons.

'Anyroad, the dog – Gronny – chased me on two legs all the way to the pond, and then when we were there she . . .' I hesitated.

'Yes, what did she do?'

'She spoke to me.'

'Still in the guise as a dog?'

'What?'

The Father sighed then explained. 'Was she still in the shape of a dog?'

'Aye.' I nodded hard, I were worried I'd gone too far then, and he were finding fault. 'Aye, she were still a dog when she spoke.'

'And what did she say?' He sounded vexed now, I thought I'd better get on with the tale.

'She told me to throw mesen into the pond. She said death in water were a calm, gentle passing. A good way to go.'

'And did you throw yourself in?'

'Oh no, Master, I don't want to die, I weren't gonna throw mesen in.'

'So what did you do?'

I looked up at the ceiling again to think. Then I had it. 'I didn't do owt, Master, I were saved.'

'And who saved you?' His eyebrows were raised again.

'I don't reetly know, but it were someone in white.'

'What, a white dress?'

'Nay, they were all ower white, like some beggar wearing a sheet ower his head. Covered him all it did.'

'I see. And what did this figure in white do?'

'Well it chased the dog, Gronny, away, and saved me.' I beamed at him and he bowed his head in thought.

'Anything else? Was my niece, Mistress Jane, with her on any of these occasions?'

I came ower all shy and shook me head. I liked Mistress Jane, even if she were a friend of Aunt Ellen, and had no reason to tell tales of her, but didn't know what I ought to do. Then I thought of summat. 'Gronny – the dog – came back when I were a couple of fields away.'

'Oh? And what did it do?'

'Took me to the ferryman's barn – Master Walshman's, that is.'

'Thomas Walshman?'

'Nay, his father, Hugh. Anyroad, the dog took me to the barn, put me ont' floor, and covered me with straw.'

'And then what?'

'It lay on top of me, and I had no speech nor senses – Gronny took 'em all.'

'That does sound frightening.'

I nodded. 'Aye, Fath— Master, it were that. Master Walshman, Thomas this is, he found me, and took me into his father's house, and I lay there some days, not moving and not talking.'

'I see. And is this the only time something like that happened?'

'Oh no, Master, it happened again it did, and not long after. I were back at the ferry and both Gronny and Aunt Ellen were there, and I fell down and couldn't speak again. Pa had to come and fetch me home.'

'Anything else?'

I shook me head. Reckon I'd said enough for one day. Would he let me go home now? There were still time to catch up with Sarah and Stevie afore dusk, and the Father had promised me some bacon to take home for supper.

'Hmm, it sounds like good and evil have been fighting for your soul for some time, child. Being still and silent in the way you describe is most definitely a sign of possession.'

'What?' I stared at him in horror.

'Do not fear, child, it does not sound as though evil has yet won out, and I shall not let it take you. You shall not become a demoniac, not while I'm here to help you, but you must do as I say. Will you do as I say, Grace?'

I bounced me head up and down. I didn't want no demons having hold of me; I knew *that* for sure.

'Good. I think we shall begin study of a new book today. Not the Good Book, but a book written by good men, nonetheless. Indeed, they were Inquisitors of the Church and stalwart men of faith.

Heinrich Kramer and Jakob Sprenger.'

I stared at him, what were he on about?

The Father forced a smile. 'I see I am confusing you. This is the book, *Malleus Maleficarum*, it means The Hammer of Witches, and is an excellent tool in the fight against witchcraft and the Devil who commands them. I think we shall begin with the evils done to children, and ensure you are not put in any further danger of corruption.'

I stared at the pages he'd opened before me. I had some letters, and could write me name, just about, but I could make no sense of these words.

'It is in Latin, child, but fear not, I shall explain to you what it teaches us.'

I sighed, then clamped me lips together when he glared at me. Gronny and Aunt Ellen would pay for this; they'd pay dear, they would.

Chapter 4

Wednesday 15th April 1612

'Here we are.' The Father jumped down from the cart and strode towards the front door of the big hall. No back door for him. I followed behind, wondering if I'd be allowed in through the front an'all.

I couldn't wait to tell me mam if I were! It were a fine hall, and all of stone, not like the hall at Samlesbury, which were larger, to be fair, but had a lot of wood with the stone. There were even glass in every window here, upstairs ones an'all, and I stared up at 'em in wonder. It were nowt like the cottage we lived in. It even had stone on its roof instead of straw!

The door opened as we approached and I jumped behind the Father and peered round him. I recognised both men standing on the stoop – they went to the Father's Mass. One were Robert Holden, the magistrate. This must be his hall then, as I knew the other man well. William Alker lived in a cottage – bigger than ours, aye, but still a cottage in Samlesbury.

Master Holden shook William's hand and he bowed to the Father in greeting as he passed. He barely looked at me.

'Robert!' the Father said and shook Master Holden's hand. I stared at them, why did they not bow like most folk did? 'Did you have success with Master Alker? What did he have to say?'

'He has confirmed what you believe, that your father liked Jane not, and did indeed fear she was a witch and would make him her victim.'

The Father nodded, his face grave. 'Poor fellow, to be tormented so deeply in his final years. Do you have enough now to arrest her?'

'Indeed I do, Master Thomson.' I caught the man's smile and wondered if he were frit an'all of the Father's wrath if he called him wrong. 'In fact, I have sent men to the Lower Hall to secure her and bring her here.'

'That is good. Although you may need to send them back into Samlesbury to pick up a couple of her demonic consorts once you hear what my young charge here has to say. Grace, this is Master Robert Holden Esquire. He will ask you some questions and you must tell him what you have told me about your grandmother and aunt, and anything else you have remembered.'

I pinched me lips tight against me groan. This were gonna be a long day of talk and questions. I just hoped I wouldn't be getting into any more trouble, Pa were vexed enough about how much time I were spending with the Father instead of helping with the stock and crops, although the extra food I brought home from the hall helped stay his temper. I sighed. I had no choice but to say it all again. At least we were inside now and out of the rain.

I told the tale about Gronny being a dog sometimes and striking me dumb and senseless then sat still and watched the Father and Master Holden. They were sitting at the other side of a table and Master Holden had a quill and paper and had been writing all the time I were talking, and kept asking me to say things again.

I reached forward and emptied me tankard of small ale. It were tasty enough, but not as strong as Mam brewed. I'd have to remember to tell her that; she'd like that hers is better.

The two men were talking, their heads together, and I thought I might as well give it a go. I reached forward, grasped the jug and filled me tankard back up. The Father glanced at me with a frown, but Master Holden didn't seem to notice. I hid me grin with the tankard as I sipped more ale.

After a while, Master Holden looked up at me. 'And how do you suppose your grandmother changed her appearance into that of a dog?'

I glanced up at the Father, who nodded. We'd

talked about this the other day, when I were learning from that horrible Inquisitors' book. There were all sorts in them pages that I didn't know were signs of witchcraft. I were truly frit now of Gronny and Aunt Ellen, and everything they did.

'Well, summat happened, about a year since, before I knew me gronny and aunt were witches.'

'Your gronny is Jennet Bierley and your aunt Ellen Bierley?'

I nodded, me lips tight. He kept asking me that, and I kept telling him. What were the point of writing it down if he didn't look back at his words? I took another sip of ale to hide me frown.

'And you are sure it was a year ago?'

'Aye, I remember it were Lent.'

Master Holden nodded and I took that as leave to carry on with the tale.

'One night they came to our cottage, and took me out with them, and we went ower the fields to Thomas Walshman's cottage; he's the ferryman.' I paused, but he didn't ask any more questions.

'Anyroad, the doors were all barred o'course, but Gronny opened them anyway—'

'How did she do that?'

'I don't know, Master, I couldn't see what she did, I were behind her.'

He nodded again, used his quill, then looked up at me.

'Well, Gronny went up the stairs to the sleeping

chamber and came back down with their babby.'

'And the parents did not wake?'

'No sir, we heard not a peep from them the whole time we were there. The babby never made noise neither. Anyroad, I were sat by the fire – even though the peat were banked up there were still a bit of warmth there – and Gronny put the babby into me arms to hold, and then . . .'

'Yes, then what did she do?'

'Well, she took a nail, an iron one she had in her apron, and thrust it into the baby's belly to make an hole.'

Master Holden were staring at me and I nodded to tell him I were serious.

'Where, exactly, did they make the hole? Can you point to the place on your own body?'

I did so and they seemed happy.

'And did the child cry?' Father Christopher asked.

'Nay, it stayed quiet.' I'd found be now that not calling him anything, or sticking to sir, were better than getting me Masters and Fathers mixed up.

'And then what happened?'

I turned back to Master Holden. 'She took a quill from her apron, bit like that un there,' I nodded at his hand, 'placed it in the hole in the babby, and did suck there a good space.'

Master Holden looked ill. Father Southworth waved his hand at me to carry on talking.

'And then Aunt Ellen did it too.'

Master Holden held his hand up while he wrote all this down, and I sipped me ale to wet me throat. All this talking were making it sore.

'And then Gronny took the babby back upstairs to its mam and pa, then they took me back home.'

'Did you suck from the baby, Grace?' Father Southworth asked.

'Oh no, sir, I did not, nothing would make me do that!'

'But you watched them do it and did not try to stop them?' Master Holden said.

I shrugged. 'They're me aunt and gronny, me elders, I were only a child, what could I do?' I weren't only a child, I'd been thirteen, but best they thought of me that way. It were better than being thought a witch too.

'What happened when you returned home?'

'Nothing, Master, me mam and pa never knew I were gone.'

'And what happened to the child?'

'Well, he were never the same after that. Allus poorly, and he passed not long after.'

'I see, and was that the end of it?'

'No, Master. After he died and were buried, Gronny and Aunt Ellen came for me again. They took me to the churchyard and we took up the babby.'

Master Holden swallowed then took a long gulp of ale. I watched the lump in his throat go up and down, up and down, and wondered if the ale were gonna come back out again.

'Which churchyard?' His voice were a croak.

'The one at Samlesbury, Master, by the river. St Leonard-the-Less.'

He took more ale and wrote this down. He didn't look up at me again, but waited, head bowed for me to tell the rest.

'We took him back to Gronny's house, and some of him she boiled in a pot, and some she roasted in the fire.' Both men looked a bit green around the gills now – but then they'd never have butchered a lamb or wrung a chicken's neck, they had others to do that for 'em. Meat is meat, as me mam allus says.

Master Holden cleared his throat. 'Did they . . . did they . . . eat—?'

'Aye, they did, Master. Not me though, I don't eat babbies and they couldn't make me.'

The men stared at me, and I rushed on. The sooner this were done, the sooner I could go home.

'They boiled the bones in a pot till they were runny and made a paste, and that's what they put on themselves to change their shape into dogs or owt else they want to look like.' I nodded to show them it were true. 'Aye, and to take flight an'all.'

Master Holden didn't ask me to say any of that again. I don't think he'd ever forget it, but he wrote it all down anyroad. I helped mesen to some more ale. Not even Father Christopher seemed to care now. Reckon I could help mesen to owt here, and they wouldn't bat an eyelid. Not after that.

* * *

'You!'

The shout came as soon as Master Holden's steward opened the front door. I jumped and tried to hide behind the Father once more as I recognised Jane Southworth. That were a mistake. She jerked away from the men holding her and flew at the Father.

'This is your doing, Christopher! Did you know they were going to arrest me in front of Thomas? He's twelve years old and watched his mother being taken away in irons!' She shook her manacled hands in his face. He leaned away from her, and I stepped round him, fearing he were going to knock me ower. I looked up at him. He were smiling.

'That was your doing, not mine, Mistress. You should not have been dabbling in witchcraft, then you would not have been arrested in front of your son.'

'You know damn well I am no witch!'

The Father frowned at her blasphemy and stared down at her. He were enjoying her distress, it were clear.

'And you!' She'd seen me. 'You stupid child! Do you have any idea what you've done? Your pa should flog you!' She slapped me and her manacles caught the side of me head and knocked me to the ground. I slipped down the steps and stared up at her, dazed. Aye, she *must* be a witch. She were as bad as Gronny and Aunt Ellen, if not worse. Were she the one that made them witches?

I knew enough to stay where I were though, and keep me mouth shut, at least until the two men had a good hold of her again.

The Father stepped ower me and bent to thrust his face into Mistress Southworth's. 'It seems you have robbed the child of her speech and senses. More proof of witchcraft.'

Mistress Southworth stared at him, her mouth open. She did not protest as the men she'd shaken off grasped her arms once more.

'Why can you not face the truth?' she said, her voice calm and sad now. 'After the Gunpowder Treason there is no room here for the Catholic faith. Far from resuscitating the Church of Rome on these shores, Fawkes and his gang have lost it to us all! The only true church in England now is the Church of England, even *you* must see that!'

The Father said nowt, but watched her being led away with a smile on his face.

Master Holden stepped forward to stand next to him. 'I'll send the men back out to fetch Jennet and Ellen Bierley, then all three shall be committed to Lancaster Castle for examination and no doubt trial at the next Assizes.'

The Father nodded, then beckoned me and walked to the cart. I followed as quietly as I could. I just wanted to go home and forget this day.

Chapter 5

Wednesday 6ᵗʰ May 1612

I hugged the haunch of beef close to me chest as I ran. Father Southworth had given it me out of his own pantry! It were well wrapped, but it were raining again and I didn't want the blood to seep out afore I got it home. I had to be quick before any bugger else saw it an'all; they'd only try and take it from me.

I near jumped down the garden steps in front of the hall, then ran along to the footpath to the village.

It were good to get out of that place, and away from him and his horrible book. I were doing so much learning, it were getting hard to keep it all straight in me head. I didn't know what were what anymore; what had really happened and what the books and the Father said might have happened.

One thing were for sure, though, he hated witches, and so he should. He'd saved me from the witches in me own family without a day to spare, that were reet enough.

I had no idea Gronny Jennet and Aunt Ellen were trying to turn me into a witch when they dragged me to their church that day. And they almost did turn me an'all. Father Christopher reckoned that if he hadn't seen me outside St Leonard's that Sunday and put me back ont' reet path, *I* would be a witch be now, dancing and cavorting with the Devil no less!

But I were safe now that they were in Lancaster Gaol; aye, and that Jane Southworth too. I put me hand to me face. I had a scar where her irons had cut me when she slapped me that day at Holden Hall. It still hadn't healed reet. I fumbled with the meat and took a proper hold on it again.

God save him, the Father did make me a bit frit, but that were just his strange ways. He were truly a man of God and must know what's best. I clambered over the stile to cut across the field to our cottage.

Oh bugger! Sarah and Stevie! What were they doing going into her Pa's barn? Were he helping her with a lamb? Or summat else? It weren't fair – why did she get hair the colour of summer wheat, and I got hair the colour of cow pats?

I twirled a dark-brown curl about me finger, then tucked the stray lock back under me cap. There weren't much I could do about it, and I turned to follow them to see what were going on, but then remembered the meat. I looked at the barn, then down at the beef. Me mouth watered, and I turned away, me tears at least hidden by rain water. Hopefully it were just a difficult lambing he were there for. He were a good lad, allus with an helping hand.

It probably *were* a lamb – it were bad how few lambs and calves had been born this spring. No bugger would be eating much meat. But then, it had been so wet and cold, there weren't that much good grass for the stock, which meant little milk for the newborns. It were mebbe a blessing that the lambings were late and few. I just hoped the rain would clear enough to let the wheat grow, we hadn't enough int' grain store for us, never mind the stock. Couldn't do owt about that, though, I had to get this meat home quick.

I slowed as I got close to the cottage. Mam and Pa were rowing again. Pa'd never liked Gronny and Aunt Ellen, and he were furious when he learned they'd taken me to their church.

Mam tried to stick up for 'em when he started on, they were her mother and sister, after all, but even she were vexed with them now.

It took them a moment to see me int' doorway, and they glared daggers at me when they did spot me. I nearly made the sign against the evil eye. But then they saw the beef and the fightin' were ower with. For now, anyroad. They were well pleased with the meat.

God bless Father Southworth.

Chapter 6

Thursday 7th May 1612

I put me hand on Master Holden's family *Bible* and swore to God I'd tell the truth, then I were allowed to sit down, have a bite of cheese, and sup some ale.

'We have covered an awful lot to date, Grace. What your grandmother and aunt did to the Walshman's baby to make their ointments . . .' He stopped then started again. 'To . . . er . . . to change their shape into dogs and the like, and the number of times you have seen them in their other shapes. Do you have anything to add?'

'Aye I do, Master. Black Sabbats. I didn't know that's what they were till the Master learned me. But I know now and I'll tell you all about 'em.'

'What do you mean you didn't know until the Master learned . . . taught you?'

Father Southworth answered him. 'We've been studying the *Malleus Maleficarum* in order to keep Grace safe from the witches who have been trying to take her soul for the use of the Devil. It turns out that she has actually experienced a Black Sabbat. More than one in fact.'

Master Holden's eyebrows shot up in alarm. Why did he believe the Father and not me? 'Really?'

'Do you have a copy of the *Malleus Maleficarum*, Robert?'

'I do not, no.'

'I have a spare copy; you can collect it at Mass on Sunday. It makes for interesting reading, and will help you and Thomas Covell as you prepare for the Summer Assizes.'

'My thanks, Christopher.'

Ha, he nearly called him Father, then. I could tell.

'You had better tell me all about it, Grace.'

'Well, last year – after the thing with Babby Walshman, but before Christmas, Gronny and Aunt Ellen came to fetch me again and we walked to Lower Hall to fetch Mistress Southworth,' I began.

'Let us be clear on this,' Father Southworth said. 'You were with Jennet and Ellen Bierley, *and* with Mistress Jane Southworth?'

'Aye sir. We did it every Thursday and Sunday night for a fortnight.'

'So this happened four times in total?' That were Master Holden asking.

'Aye, Master. Two Thursdays and two Sundays.'

'What happened once Mistress Southworth joined you?'

'Well, we crossed the river, didn't we? Went ower the water to Red Bank.'

'How did you cross over? The Ribble has been

flowing fast for some time now, and the ford is difficult to negotiate.'

I shrugged. 'There were four black things, Gronny must have called on 'em or summat. I remember, me feet were still dry, but I were ont' other bank. I were rare frit, I were.'

'I see.' Father Southworth were asking the questions now, and Master Holden were just writing. 'And what did these black things look like?'

'I dunno, it were dark and they were hard to see.' The Father frowned at me, and I hurried on. 'But they stood upright and they didn't have faces like any man.'

'What did their faces look like if they didn't look like a man's?' Master Holden asked.

I stayed quiet a bit then shrugged. 'I don't reetly know how to describe 'em. Bit like dogs, bit like goats, but not like either.' I shrugged again. They'd have to make do with that.

'And then what happened?' Father Southworth asked.

'Well, they had some sort of strange food, magical food, which they all ate, but I didn't eat it, no matter what Gronny said, all I could think on were the Walshman babby. I've never eaten owt me gronny's made since then.'

'That sounds very sensible, my girl.'

I grinned at him. 'They all ate their fill, and then when it had all gone, they danced with the black things.'

'And you, Grace, did you dance as well?'

I looked down at me lap. I couldn't look at the Father now. 'Aye, I did. I like dancing, and I'm the best dancer at May Day, and I couldn't see any harm in just dancing, we were all dancing together, and I didn't know then that they were witches.'

'Fear not, child, you are not in trouble here. Whatever you have done, you have returned to God and I have granted you absolution. You are not in danger, your soul is safe, but we do need to know it all.'

I nodded, but kept me head down. 'Well, we were all dancing, and then we all lay down on the ground. Me gronny, aunt and Mistress Jane, they were dancing on the ground with the black things.'

'Dancing on the ground?'

'Aye. They were laid down but still bumping up and down like they could hear a fiddle or a drum playing.'

The Father and Master shared a glance, and I sipped me ale to hide me smile. I couldn't let the Father know I knew all about rutting. He wouldn't like that, no matter what he'd said a minute ago.

'And what about you, Grace, did you er . . . dance on the ground with one of the black things?'

'Nay! I mean, I did lie down like I said, and the black thing that had been dancing with me, it lay on top of me and did abuse me body, but only through me clothes, I didn't do owt,' I rushed on, making sure they knew I'd not rutted.

'And what happened next?'

'Then they took us back ower the river and we went home.'

'Nothing else?' the Father said, and I looked at him, wondering what I'd forgotten, then I remembered.

'Not then, but since I came here before, Mistress Southworth has visited me a few times and taken me senses, just like Gronny Jennet used to do.'

Master Holden stopped writing and stared at me. 'But how can she visit you, Grace? She is in Lancaster Castle, and cannot get out.'

I had an answer for that one. 'She's a witch. She knows how to be in two places at once. Witches can do that you know, they're asleep in one place but appear in another.'

Father Southworth nodded his agreement and Master Holden seemed happy with that. 'When did she come to you?'

'Um, the first time were about ten days after I came here afore. She carried me to the hayloft and put me there, and Pa found me and took me back into our cottage. I had no senses till the next day, when she came again. That time she put me on top of an haystack and most of the village were looking for me afore I were found. I were dumb and couldn't move for two or three days that time.'

'Are those the only instances?' I looked at Master Holden, not sure what he meant.

'Did it happen again, Grace?' Father Southworth asked.

'Nay, not yet, but I'm frit she will do it again.'

'I see,' Master Holden said, making more words with his quill. 'I have another appointment now, but it sounds as if you'll need to come again, so we can talk about these visits in full. I've taken a note of the approximate dates and will check with the Gaoler, Master Covell, at Lancaster to see if he noticed any strange behaviour by Jane Southworth, or the other two for that matter, at those times.'

I nodded. I could do that. It weren't much fun, but they gave me plenty of ale, and food too. All I could eat – and I could eat a lot when I had a mind to.

Chapter 7

Saturday 8th August 1612

Mam went to the cottage door to whistle for Pa, but he were already on his way back from checking the ewes. The smell of roasting pigeon had reached him.

'That smells good, missus,' he said, giving Mam a pat on her backside before sitting at the table.

'Pigeons are from Holden Hall's own coop, *and* they sent blood for the black broth and some of yesterday's good white bread from the Hall's kitchen.'

'You've done well, me girl,' Pa said and I beamed – he never gave much praise out.

I sat next to him and poured his ale as Mam ladled the rich stew into our wooden bowls, before sitting down hersen.

'I had to tell everything again, and Master Holden were reading what he wrote the first time I told him, so I knew I had to get it reet. I told him about another time Mistress Jane magicked me into a fit an'all, I forgot I hadn't told him about it before, but that were all reet, as it only happened after I saw him last. He lapped it up, and the Gaoler at Lancaster even said that when Mistress Jane were magicking me, she were asleep ont' floor of her dungeon. Father Southworth were well pleased with me.' I took a breath and lifted me hand to me face again. I'd allus have the scar the witch gave me.

'John Singleton were at Holden Hall an'll, talking about how the old Master Southworth said that Jane were an evil woman and a witch and that he were sorry for her husband – his grandson – for he thought she would kill him. And her husband's dead reet enough. Apparently Old Master John wouldn't go anywhere near Lower Hall for fear of her. I reckon she'll pay for it all. The Assizes aren't long away now. That'll be the last time I'll have to tell the tales, and I'll have to tell 'em good.'

'Aye, lass, but hush now and sup up.' Pa used his eating knife to point at me pigeon, but I hadn't finished yet. I needed to tell him the next bit while he were cheerful, and having meat ont' table allus put him in a good temper.

'They might need you to stand up and tell 'em about fetching me back from Aunt Ellen's, Pa, and about Mistress Jane coming to the house and putting me in fits.'

Pa dropped his knife. 'But she'll hang! Jennet and Ellen too! Don't you see that? Whole village is talking about Jennet Preston from Gisborne hanging at York a couple of weeks back. Demdike and Chattox are in Lancaster Gaol an'all, and I don't fancy their chances much.' Pa drained his ale, picked up his knife and stabbed another bit of meat.

Everyone int' county had heard of Owd Demdike and Chattox. They'd been cursing each other for years, and plenty of other folk too. When I were little, Mam used to tell me Owd Demdike would come get me if I didn't behave mesen. And now Gronny and Aunt Ellen were keeping company with 'em!

'We have to back our Grace, or *she'll* be accused of witchcraft an'all, and they'll hang *her*, and she's done nowt to bring on this trouble. Me mam and Ellen have brought it on themselves. Sticking their noses into our business and angering the Father.' Mam's face were bright red as she railed at Pa.

'They shouldn't have taken Grace to that church and put her soul in danger, they should have left well alone, but they never can – they never could! You know what me mam's like, allus thinks she knows best, and Ellen's just as bad. Well, look where it's got 'em. Nay, they're done for with the Father against 'em. We have to look to oursens, and keep our Grace safe. I can't lose her as well as me mam and sister. We need to trust Father Southworth.'

'All you have to do is tell how you fetched me back from Aunt Ellen's a time or two when I weren't feeling well, and I weren't talking, which you know ain't like me. And then that Mistress Jane's been coming to the cottage, and where you found me after her visits.'

'Well, you were lost in that haystack, lass, that

time, and you took to your bed after I found you int'
barn, but I ain't seen Mistress Jane, you know that.'

'The Father's been very generous, Thomas,' Mam
said. 'Most of the meat we've eaten since Easter has
come from Samlesbury Hall. We could starve this
winter if he don't help us, *and* lose most of the stock
too. You have to do reet by us and back Grace's tale,
Thomas, you have to.'

Chapter 8

Tuesday 18th August 1612

Father Southworth came to see us off yesterday. He couldn't come with us – as a seminary priest, he shouldn't even be in Lancashire, and the court would exile him or worse if he turned up at the castle. He handed John Singleton a good-sized purse, though, to pay for all our lodgings and food. The Assizes proper would start today – the Father said they only swore in the juries and got ready on the Monday – but the trials would then last the week, and it looked like he were being generous with us. We'd all be eating well these next days. Mind you, he'd asked for contributions at Mass on Sunday for the fight against witchcraft, and I reckon he'd collected ten times as much as he gave to us.

He placed his hand on me head to give me his blessing. 'This is the final test of your faith, my girl,' he'd said to me. 'You succeed here and we can forever rid you of the wickedness which, through no fault of your own, has tainted your soul. I bless you in your endeavours, and know that God is with you.'

41

He made the sign of the cross and I copied him – I knew it were safe here in the grounds of Samlesbury Hall – then clambered into the back of the cart to join Mam, Pa and the others.

There were six of us in all, plus Stevie Armstrong, who had care of the horse and cart. He winked at me when I sat down on the straw bale behind him ont' driver's bench – and even better, Pa didn't see it. Ha, so much for Sarah Pickles!

It had taken all day to get here though. I hadn't realised Lancaster were so distant – I'd only been as far as Preston afore, and we stopped there for an early dinner, but it were getting dark by the time we got to Lancaster. Me backside were that sore, I could barely walk! And me mam needed Pa to help her get down from the cart. She'd never needed an arm holding for her afore.

We found an inn, comfortable enough, but we all slept together in the one room, I suppose to keep as much of the money as we could for food. Everyone were after taking some home with us as well as what we ate here, and I reckon we'd have slept in the cart if we'd not needed to look fair for the courtroom. I didn't mind sharing a room though. We all had pallets of straw, and I managed to get the one next to Stevie. But Pa put paid to that when he put himself and Mam betwixt the two of us.

We stayed wakeful through the night though, and whispered together once Mam and Pa had started snoring. Stevie weren't daft enough to try owt else with Pa int' room, but it were good to be talking with him again. Once this week were done, I wouldn't have to go to Father Southworth's for learning no more either and I'd see more of Stevie at home too.

We'd seen the lights of the castle up on the hill as we drove into Lancaster Monday night, the flames of torches flickering up the high stone walls, and the sight had quietened us all, so I knew it were big, but when we rounded the corner on our way from the inn after a good break-fast, the sheer size of it took me breath away. I'd never seen owt like it and it struck me dumb.

I followed Pa ower the ditch bridge to the gatehouse – all by itself, it must have been three times the size of Holden Hall, with tall, narrow windows. I didn't know it were possible to build that big. Then I peered through and saw even taller towers within! I stepped back a pace or two, straight into Stevie Armstrong's hands.

I looked up and squinted at what looked like iron spikes hanging above me head, and froze in frit. Stevie, bless him, took me arm and led me forward, out from under it. 'It's called a portcullis,' he said, speaking the strange word slowly. 'It's like a big iron gate to stop attacking armies taking the castle.'

I peered round in alarm and he laughed. 'Don't

fret, Gracie—' I liked it when he called me Gracie '—
no bugger attacks castles no more, not since the
battles with the Scots, and that were hundreds of
years ago, and I can't see it happening again anytime
soon.'

He grinned at me smile. He went to the free
school at Blackburn every Wednesday, a two-hour
walk from Samlesbury – and drove folk mad with all
his questions. He knew such a lot about the world;
more than I could ever hope to, no matter how much
learning I did.

Presently, the Gaoler, Master Thomas Covell,
came to greet us, then escorted us to the Crown Court
in the hall next to the big square tower they called the
keep. It were reet dark inside, despite its great size,
with panelled walls and a high ceiling open to the
rafters, and were filled with wooden benches and
railings. I reckoned there were more people in the
one room here than there were in the whole of
Samlesbury.

We sat where he put us and waited, shuffling on
our seats and wondering what were going to happen
first. It felt like a big, fancy mummers' show, and I
craned me neck as some men walked in, then I
followed everyone else in standing up. I were the last
to sit down again, as I wanted a reet good look, and
Mam pulled me sleeve to bring me back to mesen,
then hooked the hair out of me mouth. That didn't
last long, I allus sucked on it when I were nervy.

I don't know why, but I thought they'd call me own name first, but that were not so.

A group of women in irons shuffled to the large box which Stevie whispered were the dock. He reckoned there were a branding iron reet there, to mark any bugger found guilty but not sent to the gallows, and I wondered if it would smell the same as when we burnt the marks into the Master's bullocks, and if everyone could smell it in such a large space, or just hear the poor buggers cry out when the heat hit their skin. I shook mesen. I were getting maudlin, that wouldn't do, I were here as witness, not accused. I spat me hair out of me mouth mesen, feeling bad about chewing it now, but not knowing why.

By the time I looked back at the women, they were being led out again. I'd missed it all.

'Pled guilty,' Stevie whispered, knowing me well enough to see when me thoughts had wandered.

They wandered most of the day as more and more people were led to the dock, me name were never called, and we just sat and watched. But at least I were sat with Stevie.

Chapter 9

Wednesday 19th August 1612

'Jennet Bierley, Ellen Bierley and Jane Southworth of Samlesbury, in the County of Lancaster, you are charged that each of you has feloniously practised, exercised and used diverse devilish and wicked arts, called witchcrafts, enchantments, charms and sorceries in and upon one Grace Sowerbutts. How plead you?'

They all said not guilty – well, o'course they would, wouldn't they? Then I were called on to stand up and point out Gronny, Aunt Ellen and Mistress Jane. The look Gronny gave me were fit to freeze me blood and I couldn't keep her eye. I were sore happy to sit again where Gronny and Aunt Ellen couldn't see me so clear.

Thomas Covell stood and greeted the judge and the other men sat with him, and now I knew why Master Holden had used his quill so much. Every word I'd said, Master Covell said now to the judge. I hadn't realised he'd pass on *everything*, even the stuff about Walshman's babby. I could feel Thomas

Walshman's eyes digging into me back, but I couldn't turn and look at him, not even Father Southworth would be able to make me do that.

The judge – Bromley his name were – listened to it all, using his own quill to make some notes. He stared hard at me a few times as Master Covell were speaking, and I looked away. But then I saw Gronny were still glaring at me too and I cast me eyes down again so I didn't have to look back. His gaze made me uncomfortable, it did – he reminded me of Father Southworth – and Gronny's were even worse.

When Master Covell had finished, the whole room – with all them people – were quiet as a churchyard, and sweat trickled down me back. Suddenly I weren't so sure that all the fuss and food that Father Southworth had given us were worth it.

I took in a deep breath when Master Covell sat down, sure the judge would be asking me questions as Father Southworth had warned me he would, but he didn't. He asked Gronny, Aunt Ellen and Mistress Jane instead, what they had to say in reply.

Well, they made a reet fuss, they did; it were shaming to witness. They fell to their knees, their hands clasped in pleading to the judge, all three of 'em weeping like babes.

I stared at the floor the whole time. Father Southworth hadn't warned me of *this*.

They said I were but a pawn in another's vendetta – I think that were the word Mistress Jane used, an ill wishing I reckon she meant – and I'd been led astray and encouraged by another.

Well, it were clear who they were talking about, but I would not lift me eyes to theirs. Nothing on earth could make me. I could feel the judge's eyes burning into me and I didn't know what to do with mesen.

Then I were knocked forward and nearly fell. Pa and Thomas Walshman were fighting! Int' court, no less, with me Mam screaming at the pair of 'em! We all backed away to give 'em room, and William Alker and John Singleton tried to break 'em up, but they couldn't, not until the bailiff waded in with his cudgel.

Well, it were a reet to do! The judge were red in his face, banging his little mallet ont' bench in front of him – I'm not sure what good he thought that would do – but everyone were calming down int' face of bailiff's cudgel, and soon it were quiet again.

'Grace Sowerbutts.' That were the judge calling me name again. He said it twice more, and Mam elbowed me to look up at him.

'It seems clear that there is more to this case than the evidence you gave to Master Holden.'

I shrugged but kept me mouth shut.

'Did you tell Master Holden the truth?'

'Aye sir,' I mumbled.

'Speak up, girl!'

I stared back at him now. 'Aye, sir,' I said.

'You will address me as Your Honour.'

Oh aye, I'd forgotten that. I shrank against Mam, frit now of what were happening. This were not like the Father had said it would be at all.

The judge stared at me in silence a while, but I wouldn't say no more.

'Has somebody told you to tell these tales?'

I stayed dumb. I were good at that when I needed to be, I took after Pa that way. It allus befuddled people when I wouldn't speak, as I were usually over fond of words. Or the sound of me own voice as Gronny oft complained. Allus telling me to hush, she were. Happen them days were ower now.

'Answer me, girl!'

I jumped. I realised I'd have to say summat or he wouldn't let up. 'I – I were sent to a Master to learn, Your Honour, that's all.'

'Learn what?'

'Me prayers, that's all. He don't have nothing to do with this, Your Honour.' That were true enough, Father Southworth hadn't told me what to say. He'd just been learning me from that book. And if I weren't careful, he'd be getting into trouble an'all, and then God knew what would befall me.

'Prayers?'

I nodded.

'Aye, from the *Bible*, and mall, mall summat or other 'bout witches and hammers.'

Judge Bromley stared at me. 'The *Malleus Maleficarum*?'

'Aye sir, Your Honour, that's it.' I nodded again to show him I were sure.

'Her Master is my late husband's uncle, Your Honour,' Jane Southworth said into the silence. 'He is a Jesuit and has recently returned to Samlesbury after many years detained at Queen Elizabeth's pleasure.'

'I see.' He sat back and sniffed, still staring at me. 'I thought I caught the smell of Popery in this. What is this priest's name?'

'Father Christopher Southworth, Your Honour, although he also uses the name Master Thomson.'

'And is he here today, Mistress?'

'I do not see him, Your Honour.'

'Why would he teach this girl these detestable accusations?'

'When he was last in Samlesbury, we were all of the old faith, Your Honour, but now come to church, and have done so for many years. Christopher likes that not.'

'I see.' He nodded with a frown at Mistress Jane. 'Well, if a priest or Jesuit has a hand in one end of it, there would appear to be knavery and practise in the other.'

He paused, and glanced at Mam and Pa. 'Who is the Master who taught your daughter? Is he this Father Southworth, or Master Thomson?'

Pa squared his shoulders. 'I know not, Your Honour.'

The judge frowned at him, but Pa wouldn't say no more. And when Pa didn't want to talk, nowt could make him.

I shuffled me feet, as it seemed every bugger else were doing, waiting for one of 'em to speak. At last, Judge Bromley gave up on Pa.

'It is clear to me that there is more to this case than has been presented.'

Master Covell went red under the judge's black look, but knew enough to stay quiet.

'Witchcraft is a scourge that has swept this county, and I shall not stand for it. But nor shall I stand for Papists accusing innocents of such wickedness, nor of using such young and simple minds to do so.'

I frowned. Who were he calling simple? Mam elbowed me and I knew she were reet. Best to say nowt.

'I am not convinced of the veracity of the evidence we have heard this day. I therefore adjourn this case, and commit Mistress Sowerbutts to be examined by my colleagues and Justices of the Peace, William Leigh and Edward Chisnal, away from all other influences, until we get to the truth of the matter.'

He banged his little mallet again, and I stared. *What?*

Gronny, Aunt Ellen and Mistress Jane were taken away from the dock, and the bailiff caught me arm and pulled me to the door.

I stared back at Mam as I went, and cursed Father Southworth under me breath.

Chapter 10

Wednesday 19th August 1612

I'd been frit of Father Southworth but that were nowt
to how frit I were now as I were pointed to a seat at
some boards in the room I were led to, and I sat
before the two men I'd seen in the courtroom, but
had paid no mind to. They looked learned and dour
in black hose and doublets. They wore no lace nor
frippery of any kind, and I doubted they'd ever
learned to smile.

'I am Master Edward Chisnal, JP, and this is
Master William Leigh, JP. You may not know it, but
Master Leigh here is not only a rector in the King's
true church, but a trusted acquaintance of the King
and was previously tutor to the Prince of Wales. We
are both appointed by King James to this Court, and
as such if you lie to us you are lying to your King. Will
you place your hand on the King's own *Bible*, and
swear to tell the truth here?'

'I so swear,' I said, me voice as quiet as an
hedgehog's sneeze as I put me hand on the book and
stared at the man who were tutor to Prince Henry. It
were his turn to speak.

'So, Mistress Sowerbutts, you must tell us the truth as you have sworn to do. Firstly, I ask you whether you truly witnessed the three you have accused of witchcraft, killing the child of Thomas Walshman with a nail in the navel, and of boiling, eating and oiling the child, thereby to transform themselves into diverse shapes?'

'Nay, Master,' I tried to say, but no words came out.

'Speak up, child!'

I flinched at the force of his voice, and felt tears pricking me eyes. I blinked them back. I hated weeping.

'You must speak!' His voice grew ever louder and I cleared me throat. I were in sore want of a sup of ale, but there were none here.

'Nay, Master,' I said at last. 'I did not witness that, nay.'

'So why did you give sworn evidence that you *had* witnessed such vile acts?'

I blinked furiously, but it weren't working, and tears ran down me cheeks, and I sobbed. 'It weren't my fault!' The words came out broken and mixed with strange noises from me throat, but they understood.

The man who had spoken first, Chisnal, snapped his fingers at the bailiff, who were stood by the door, and they waited for me to calm mesen.

A beaker of ale were put before me and I drank.

'Tell us what happened, Mistress Sowerbutts,' Master Leigh said, his dark eyes boring into me soul, and I nodded.

'Father Southworth has done wrong by me, Aunt Ellen and Gronny, I see that now.' I wiped me face with me hands as the words came out a mite easier.

'So Father Southworth is indeed Master Thomson?'

'Aye, Master, they're the same man, reet enough. Mam sent me to him to learn me prayers.'

'And what form did these lessons take?' Master Leigh were asking the questions with Master Chisnal writing down me answers. It were just like being at Holden Hall, though the ale weren't as good.

'We did learning from the *Bible* and other books, and he learned me all about witches and witchcrafts, and he made me think Gronny and Aunt Ellen were witches, and then he made me think Mistress Jane were a witch an'all. *And* he made me learn all about eating babbies and dancing with Devils and looking like dogs, and it's been reet fearsome it has, Master, I been so frit.' I stopped, gasping for breath as Master Leigh raised an hand at me. I took a sup of ale and me breath slowed and grew regular again.

'But you did not see any of that, only heard about it from Father Southworth?'

'Aye, Master, that's reet. He put them pictures in me head he did, and he made me tell of 'em.'

'And what of these . . . fits you, your father and

Master Walshman have spoken of?'

I looked down at me hands again. 'Father Southworth made me think them had happened an'all.'

'I see. So you were not cast upon any haystack nor into any barn?'

'Nay, Master, I weren't.' I swallowed some more ale to wet me throat. 'I went up on the haystack mesen, as I didn't want to do me chores. I were hiding from me mam.'

The man stared at me, without once blinking, and I could feel me cheeks go red and more tears ready themselves to fall.

Once Chisnal finished writing, they whispered together, then Master Chisnal spoke.

'We shall now speak with Mistress Southworth and the two Mistresses Bierley to hear what they have to say about the matters at hand. You shall go back to the courtroom, Mistress Sowerbutts, and await this new evidence which we shall present to the judge in due course.'

I stared at them. 'Have I done reet?'

'You have done much wrong, child. I pray that God can forgive you your trespasses, but you must work hard to convince him you are truly repentant.'

'Aye, Master, I will, I will that.' I nodded me head many times to show him I meant it and then the bailiff took me away again and back to the courtroom.

I were reet glad to see Stevie Armstrong smile at me, but every bugger else looked away when I sat back down. Even Mam.

Chapter 11

Wednesday 19th August 1612

'Gentlemen of the Jury, you have heard as have I, the convoluted tales of this young girl, who has been wickedly misused and influenced by the aforesaid Father Christopher Southworth. It is now your duty to consider all you have heard in the case against Mistress Jane Southworth, Mistress Jennet Bierley and Mistress Ellen Bierley, and to acquit them of all charges.'

The jurymen huddled together and after a short whisper, one stood to declare them not guilty.

'Mistress Southworth, Mistresses Bierley, you are free to go, and I am deeply saddened for all you have endured. I wish you well in future.'

Judge Bromley banged his mallet, then carried on talking.

'I want this bloody butcher, Father Christopher Southworth, found, arrested and held to account for the crime he has attempted to use this court to commit. I shall not be used by a priest, nor any man, to commit an injustice, and should dearly like to see him standing before me at that barre at a future Assizes.

'As for you, Grace Sowerbutts, I allow you have been used badly, manipulated by a powerful man, and your innocent mind corrupted for evil doing. Let me ask you this, do you attend the church?'

'No, not by me own will, never!' Then I remembered. Everything had changed. It were Father Southworth's Mass that were wrong, not Gronny's church. 'But I will, Your Honour, I promise. I'll go to every service at Gronny's church!'

The judge smiled at me. 'Then we have done good work here today, and saved a soul for Our Good Lord.'

He looked ower at Mam and Pa. 'I charge your mother and father to regularly attend the parish church with you, and task them to take better care of you; and especial care in choosing the people given the charge of tutorship over you. Also to take serious and punitive steps to moderate your flights of fancy.'

I didn't like the sound of that last bit. Not at all.

He turned his eyes back to me. 'The occurrences of this day should serve as the most important lesson of your life, Mistress Sowerbutts. You must never forget what has happened in this courtroom. In fact, I shall make *sure* you do not forget.' He stopped for a bit, thinking.

'I command you to attend the hangings on Lancaster Moor on the morrow to witness first-hand the consequences your actions may have led to for your family and Mistress Southworth. Never forget, my girl, never forget.'

I went ice cold. I'd never seen an hanging afore. And for all me big talk with Stevie Armstrong, I didn't want to see one now.

'Although—' I chilled further as he gave me a wicked smile '—I am sure your grandmother and aunt will never allow you to forget.'

Good Lord Above, Gronny'll give me hell when we get home. And what will the Father say? Ruddy hell, what it they arrest him *next? Will I have to do all this again? Will they make me speak against him, with him stood there, listening? Watching me?*

I curled a lock of hair into me mouth. *What should I do? Where could I go?*

I jumped as Stevie took me hand in comfort. I smiled at him. *Would he take me somewhere safe? That'd be all reet, that would. Getting away from Pendle and all the talk of witches. Ooh, and having lots of adventures with Stevie Armstrong!* I shuffled closer to him, ignoring Mam's scowl.

The End

A Note on the Characters

Stevie Armstrong and Sarah Pickles are wholly fictional characters. Every other character in *Divided by Witchcraft* is based on the real life people whose evidence the court clerk, Thomas Potts, recorded at the trial of Jane Southworth, Jennet Bierley and Ellen Bierley on 19th August, 1612, and subsequently published in *The Wonderful Discovery of Witches in the County of Lancaster*.

Divided by Witchcraft is the second in a new series of historical fiction short stories examining the frenzy of witch hunting that swept the north of England in the late 16th and early 17th centuries – including the most famous, that of the Pendle Witches in 1612.

You are very welcome to join Karen in her Facebook readers' group to see the news about upcoming events and releases first, and to discuss and share your thoughts and/or questions about any of Karen's fiction:
www.facebook.com/groups/karenperkinsbookgroup

For more information on the full range of Karen Perkins' fiction, please visit Karen's website:
www.karenperkinsauthor.com

Acknowledgements

My thanks to Celia Marshall, a descendent of the Southworth family, who gave me her blessing to write this story – your support and encouragement is very much appreciated, Celia, and I sincerely hope I have done Jane Southworth, as well as Jennet and Ellen Bierley, justice. Thankfully, they did receive some justice in life, albeit after suffering an horrific ordeal.

I am very grateful to my good friend and editor, Louise Burke – I rely on you to save my blushes and you never disappoint!

To family, friends and most importantly, thank you, Dear Reader. The posts, comments, messages and reviews you share with me, whether in person, on social media or on Amazon and Goodreads lift me, motivate me, and are so very much appreciated. There is no better feeling for an author than to know people enjoy her books.

If you would like to find out more about the events that inspired *Divided by Witchcraft*, the following books make for fascinating reading:

Almond PC (2012) *The Lancashire Witches: A Chronicle of Sorcery and Death on Pendle Hill*, I.B.Taurus, London

Borman T (2014) *Witches: James I and the English Witch-Hunts*, Vintage, Random House, London

Lumby J (1995) *The Lancashire Witch-Craze: Jennet Preston and the Lancashire Witches, 1612*, Carnegie Publishing Ltd, Lancaster

Maxwell-Stuart P.G. (2007) *The Malleus Maleficarum Selected, translated and annotated by P.G. Maxwell-Stuart*, Manchester University Press, Manchester

Poole R (2011) *The Wonderful Discovery of Witches in the County of Lancaster*, Palatine Books, Lancaster.

More Books by Karen Perkins

The Yorkshire Ghost Stories

Ghosts of Thores-Cross
The Haunting of Thores-Cross: A Yorkshire Ghost
Story
Cursed: A Yorkshire Ghost Short Story
JENNET: now she wants the children

Ghosts of Haworth
Parliament of Rooks: Haunting Brontë Country

Ghosts of Knaresborough
Knight of Betrayal: A Medieval Haunting

To find out more about the full range of Yorkshire
Ghost Stories, including upcoming titles, please visit:
www.karenperkinsauthor.com/yorkshire-ghosts

The Great Northern Witch Hunts
Murder by Witchcraft: A Pendle Witch Short Story
Divided by Witchcraft: Inspired by the true story of
the Samlesbury Witches

To find out more about the full range of books in the
Great Northern Witch Hunts series, please visit:
www.karenperkinsauthor.com/pendle-witches

The Valkyrie Series
Historical Caribbean Nautical Adventure
Look Sharpe! (Book #1)
Ill Wind (Book #2)
Dead Reckoning (Book #3)

The Valkyrie Series: The First Fleet (Look Sharpe!, Ill
Wind & Dead Reckoning)

To find out more about the full range of books in the
Valkyrie Series, please visit:
www.karenperkinsauthor.com/valkyrie

About the Author

Karen Perkins is the author of the Yorkshire Ghost Stories, the Pendle Witch Short Stories and the Valkyrie Series of historical nautical fiction. All of her fiction has appeared at the top of bestseller lists on both sides of the Atlantic, including the top 21 in the UK Kindle Store in 2018.

Her first Yorkshire Ghost Story – THE HAUNTING OF THORES-CROSS – won the Silver Medal for European Fiction in the prestigious 2015 Independent Publisher Book Awards in New York, whilst her Valkyrie novel, DEAD RECKONING, was long-listed in the 2011 MSLEXIA novel competition.

Originally a financial advisor, a sailing injury left Karen with a chronic pain condition which she has been battling for over twenty five years (although she did take the European ladies title despite the injury!). Writing has given her a new lease of – and purpose to – life, and she is currently working on *A Question of Witchcraft* – a sequel to *Parliament of Rooks: Haunting Brontë Country*, as well as more Pendle Witch short stories.

To find out more about current writing projects as well as special offers and competitions, you are very welcome to join Karen in her Facebook group. This is an exclusive group where you can get the news first, as well as have access to early previews and chances to get your hands on new books before anyone else.

Find us on Facebook at:
www.facebook.com/groups/karenperkinsbookgroup

See more about Karen Perkins, including contact details and sign up to her newsletter, on her website:
www.karenperkinsauthor.com

Karen is on Social Media:

Facebook:
www.facebook.com/karenperkinsauthor
www.facebook.com/Yorkshireghosts
www.facebook.com/groups/karenperkinsbookgroup

Twitter:
@LionheartG

Instagram:
@yorkshireghosts

www.ingramcontent.com/pod-product-compliance
Lightning Source LLC
Chambersburg PA
CBHW020601030426
42337CB00013B/1159